God's
little book of
Peace

Words of peace and inspiration
for weary souls

Richard Daly

D1460781

Collins

Collins, a division of
HarperCollins Publishers
77–85 Fulham Palace Road

First published in Great Britain in 2007
© 2007 Richard Daly

Richard Daly asserts the moral right to be identified as the author
of this work

A catalogue record for this book is available from the British
Library

ISBN-13: 978-0-00-724624-3

Printed and bound in Great Britain by
Martins the Printers, Berwick upon Tweed
Typeset by MATS Typesetters, Southend-on-Sea, Essex

INTRODUCTION

In a world where distress and anxiety have
become the norms, how can we truly experience
peace in a peaceless world?

Harmony amongst nations and between people
struck by terror and disaster is hard to come by.
Yet in the midst of turmoil, peace can still be
achieved. It is possible to live in a world without
peace, and yet still be in peace. Such an
experience comes only from knowing God.

This little volume is designed to provide you
with insightful words to help you discover
true peace for yourself.

Open this book at any page and be inspired.

Richard Daly

KNOW GOD, KNOW PEACE ...
NO GOD, NO PEACE

One of the many titles given to God is
'Jehovah-Shalom' which means the 'God of Peace'.
Our first step in finding true peace
is in getting to know God.

Judges 6:24

WISH PEACE

The Jewish word for peace is Shalom. Its meaning
signifies a deep inner wellbeing that is often wished
upon someone in greeting. Greet someone today in
this way and wish peace into their life.

Daniel 4:1

GET CONNECTED

The greatest quest in life has always been the
search for peace. Many have travelled far and
wide, yet the path to peace is a direct line
between God and man ... the oneness
of divinity and humanity.

Jeremiah 29:13

THINK TRANQUILLITY

Tranquillity – what a peaceful word. Picture
yourself in a tranquil scene – by a calm flowing
river, a serene sunset, a quiet meadow.
This in itself aids peace of mind.

Philippians 4:7

SEEK A PEACEFUL REMEDY

It's not work that wears us out, but worry, anxiety, stress, fear and everything else that perplexes our minds. Inner peace is the only antidote that banishes these negative emotions.

Colossians 3:15

PURSUE PEACE

Worry is something you permit; peace
is something you pursue.
That means you can learn to control
what goes on in your mind.

John 14:7

THINK PEACEFUL THOUGHTS

Agitation! Frustration! Complication! Just the
thought of these gives a sense of unrest. Calm,
Tranquillity, Serenity ... now doesn't
that just feel better?

Philippians 4:8

CLEAR YOUR CONSCIENCE

What greater peace of mind can be achieved than
when you know you are doing God's will?

Isaiah 48:18
Ephesians 5:17

GOD IS BIG!

To worry is to say to God, 'You're not big
enough to solve this problem, so I'll deal
with it myself'. Remember, you don't have
a problem He can't solve.

Psalm 24:8
Psalm 121

KNOW YOUR LIMITS

Peace disappears when you try to do something
about something you can't do anything about!

Matthew 19:26
Genesis 18:14

DELEGATE YOUR WORRIES

Ninety-two per cent of what we worry about,
we have no control over. Give the other eight
per cent to God and bask in peace of mind.

Psalms 55:22
1 Peter 5:7

KILL OVERWORK, NOT YOURSELF

If you make your work more important than
yourself, you won't be around to finish it.

Matthew 11:28-30
Romans 14:17

LIVE PEACE

'Let peace rule': that ought to be your motto!

Colossians 3:15
Isaiah 55:12

TAKE A BREAK

Never feel guilty about taking a break – God
didn't. Time taken in rest replenishes your
soul and aids a peaceful spirit.

Hebrews 4:3-5

EXPERIENCE HEAVEN IN HELL

When all hell is breaking loose around you,
yet you remain calm and confident, you're
experiencing the peace of God that
transcends all understanding.

Philippians 4:7

JUST PRAY

Inner peace need not be all that elusive.
Just pray for it.

Philippians 4:6, 7
Jeremiah 29:7

CHANGE YOUR MIND

Don't waste time focusing on things you can't
change. Instead focus on things you can, like your
perspective and attitude toward life.

Isaiah 26:3

LIVE FOR TODAY

Live one peaceful day at a time. Remember,
yesterday is gone and tomorrow is unborn;
all you have is today.

Matthew 6:25
Matthew 6:11

LOOK TO THIS DAY

Today well lived makes every yesterday a dream of
happiness and every tomorrow a vision of hope.

Psalm 118:24
2 Corinthians 6:2

WORK THROUGH YOUR PROBLEMS

Whatever problem is destroying your peace,
ask: What is the worst that can possibly happen?
Then prepare to accept it, and peacefully
proceed to improve on the worst.

Romans 8:28, 31

FEAR NOT

Fear is the opposite of peace.

1 John 4:18

BE REJUVENATED

Peacefulness promotes the most relaxing
recreating forces – good health, good sleep,
laughter and happiness.

Isaiah 58:8

SEEK WISDOM IN PROVERBS

'Don't cross your bridges before you come to them' and 'don't cry over spilt milk' are two old proverbs that can lead to a peaceful life.

Romans 12:16

THINK PEACE, GAIN PEACE

Think miserable thoughts and be miserable.
Think fearful thoughts and be fearful.
Think peaceful thoughts and be peaceful.
You are what you think!

2 Corinthians 10:5
Proverbs 23:7

DON'T HOLD GRUDGES

To forgive is a powerful release of pent-up feelings.
It leads to freedom. Freedom leads to peace.

2 Corinthians 2:7
Romans 12:17

BE GRATEFUL

Be grateful for what you have. A spirit of
appreciation goes a long way to peaceful feelings.

Ephesians 5:20
Job 1:21
Hebrews 13:5

COUNT YOUR BLESSINGS

It's not until something is taken away from you
that you realise its importance. Count your
blessings, not your troubles.

Ephesians 1:3
Hebrews 13:5

TURN YOUR MINUS TO PLUS

One of the traits of having a peaceful character is
the ability to turn unpleasant experiences into
positive lessons. Start doing that today.

Jeremiah 31:13
Psalm 30:5

BE INTERESTED IN OTHERS

In whatever problem you experience, there's always someone worse off than you. Discover other people's plights; it may make yours pale into insignificance.

Psalm 41:1
Proverbs 14:21
Galatians 6:2

SPREAD PEACE

Peace is contagious. Live peacefully and
it will rub off on people around you.

Isaiah 52:7-9

SEEK RECONCILIATION

When you are at peace with others, you will
ultimately be at peace with yourself.

Hebrews 12:14
Matthew 5:23-24

TELL GOD EVERYTHING!

The hymn writer says:
Oh what peace we often forfeit,
Oh what needless pain we bear
All because we do not carry
Everything to God in prayer.

Matthew 7:7, 8
John 14:13, 4

UNBURDEN YOUR HEART

Any psychiatrist will tell you it is therapeutic to
share your problems. If you can't tell anyone
trustworthy, you can always trust God.

Jeremiah 33:3
Isaiah 59:1

REPRODUCE PEACE

Peace begets peace. Each day ask God to help
you become an instrument of his peace.

Nahum 1:15

BE STILL

The very word peace emits a sense of stillness.
Just being still long enough will give you
a vision of what peace can be.

Psalms 46:10

BE OF ONE MIND

Worry comes from the Greek word meaning to
'divide the mind'. Peace counteracts that and
restores your mind to oneness.

Philippians 4:2
Luke 12:29-31

SPEAK TRUTHFULLY

Honesty is still the best policy and leads to inner
contentment. Deception, falsity and even half-
truths will stifle your search for peace.

John 8:32
Philippians 4:8

RELAX

It has been clinically proven that any nervous or emotional state fails to exist in the presence of complete relaxation. Make time to relax today.

Psalms 37:7-11

TAKE A POWER NAP

Rest is not doing 'nothing'. Rest is repair.
A five-minute nap during the day will
help restore peaceful vitalities.

Mark 6:31-32

HOPE

There are many people living with no hope.
Hope gives you purpose and direction;
it is the oil that fuels peace.

Romans 15:13

SEEK FORGIVENESS

Ultimate peace begins when we have peace with
God. Regardless of your past, He is willing to
forgive and forget. Just ask Him.

Romans 5:1
1 John 1:9

APPRECIATE YOURSELF

Peace is also dependent on how we feel
about ourselves. A routine of exercise
generates a feel good factor.

Ephesians 5:29

EAT HEALTHILY

Are you eating properly? If you aren't,
it will affect your energy levels, your moods
and, hence, your peace.

1 Corinthians 6:19, 20
Ephesians 5:29

PACE YOURSELF

Stress wears down your immune system and makes
you vulnerable to the very things you fear.

Proverbs 19:2

TRUST IN GOD

Trust is the highest form of faith because it doesn't need to know all the answers ... trust God and let peace take over.

Proverbs 3:5-6
2 Samuel 22:3

BE CONTENT

It is better to be content with little than anxious
having too much. Peace is not about what
or who you are, but how you are.

Luke 3:14

JUST SAY NO

The demands of life can be overwhelming.
In order for peace to flourish, learn to say 'no'.

Galatians 5:22, 23

ACCEPT HIS LOVE

No matter how unworthy you feel today, nothing
can shut off God's flowing love for you.

Songs of Solomon 8:7
John 3:16

BELIEVE GOD!

God's opinion of you, and His opinion alone,
is the only reliable basis on which to build your
self-worth. Never forget that!

Isaiah 43:1, 2
Psalm 139 1-24

RELAX YOUR MUSCLES

Right now, unless your entire body is as limp
as an old rag doll, you are at this very
moment producing nervous and muscular
tensions. Relax, relax, relax.

Psalm 46:10

MAKE PEACE A HABIT

Tension is a habit. Relaxing is a habit. Bad habits
can be broken, good habits can be developed.

Ephesians 5:15

AVOID A 'MUST DO' ATTITUDE

What limits peace? A sense of 'must' or
'obligation'; the unending list of things ahead
that simply have to be done!

Ecclesiastes 3:1-9

READ PSALM 23

Psalm 23 provides a wonderful picture of
tranquillity and peace: 'He leads me to lie down
in green pastures, he leads me beside still waters,
he restores my soul'.

Psalm 23

LET OTHERS JUDGE

You will instinctively know if you are in a state
of peacefulness and those around you will know,
too ... including your dog!

Matthew 5:16

LET GOD HEAL

Broken relationships can often lead to broken
hearts. God promises to heal the broken hearted.
Not only does He heal, He also restores.

Psalm 147:3
Psalm 145:14, 15
Jeremiah 30:17

FORGIVE OTHERS

Forgiving others not only releases you, it frees the offender. Both of you can then move on in life.

Mark 9:50

MAKE PEACEFUL CHOICES

Major decisions in life often cause anxiety.
Avoid it by taking time to pray and seek godly
counsel before you proceed.

Jeremiah 29:11-13

BE A MEDIATOR

Mediation involves being a 'go-between'
for two people in need. It is the ultimate
way to become a peacemaker.

Matthew 5:9
Ephesians 4:2-4

EMBRACE GOD'S PEACE

World peace is very much an illusion.
But with the peace of God, you can live
peacefully in a peaceless world.

John 14:27

GO SOMEWHERE PEACEFUL

To evoke peace go to a place of peace: a quiet
garden; beside a babbling brook – any place
where your soul can be uplifted.

Isaiah 32:18
1 Timothy 2:2

WISH PEACE TO OTHERS

Keep praying for peace in war-torn countries.
Your prayers could be their only hope.

Luke 10:5

SPIRITUALITY LEADS TO PEACE

The Bible counsels that to have our minds
'on the world' leads to death, but to be
spiritually-minded leads to peace and life.

Romans 8:6

SLOW DOWN

The tempo of modern life is not conducive
to rest and relaxation. Slow down! There's
no one winner in the race of life.

1 Corinthians 9:24-27

HOLD ON

When you're at your lowest point and everything
you've tried has failed, don't throw in the
towel – you may be closer to a breakthrough
than what you think!

Isaiah 54:17

ACTUALISE

Talk peaceful to be peaceful.

Colossians 4:6

LEAVE IT TO GOD

What you can't accomplish by worrying
all night, God can accomplish in an instant
by his spoken word.

Psalms 46:6, 7

LIVE PEACEABLY

There is calmness when life is lived
in gratitude and quiet joy.

Psalm 107:29, 30

SPEAK PEACEFULLY

Your words are like nitro-glycerine: they
can either blow up bridges or heal hearts.
Be careful what you say; in your tongue lays
the power for life or death.

Romans 12:18
Isaiah 50:4-7

DON'T LOSE YOUR PEACE

Next time you get all worked up, ask yourself:
What is the enemy trying to do?
His plan is to steal your joy.

Exodus 14:14
Job 13:5

CONTROL YOUR THOUGHTS

Direct your thoughts to those virtues that inspire
you – hope, joy, love and thankfulness.

Jeremiah 29:11
Luke 24:38, 39

BITTER TO SWEETNESS

Betrayal is something others do to you. Bitterness
is something you develop yourself! Look past the
hurt and you'll see that your resentment is just
a roadblock to your own peace.

Ephesians 4:31
Hebrews 12:15

GUARD YOUR MIND!

We are encouraged to 'take captive every
thought and make it obedient to Christ'.
When we actively police our minds, our defence
will begin to grow strong.

2 Corinthians 5:10

BE AT PEACE WITH YOURSELF

When you withhold forgiveness you hurt
yourself more – much more!
It hangs over you like a cloud, affecting
everything you do. Forgiveness releases peace
and restoration. So forgive today!

Matthew 6:12
1 Kings 8:50

LOVE IN ACTION

All genuine works of love are works of peace.
So keep loving.

Matthew 5:44
Luke 6:35

BE HONEST

If you always tell the truth, you never have to
worry about remembering what you said.
Nothing is more important that credibility.
Lose that and you can lose everything.

Romans 12:17

SMILE AWHILE

Peace starts with a smile. It's as simple as that!

Numbers 6:26

ENCOURAGE SOMEONE TODAY

One basic human need is to be appreciated. We all
think wonderful things about people but never tell
them. Praise becomes valuable only when you
impart it. Tell someone today how much
you appreciate them.

Romans 12:6-8

PEACE BEGETS PEACE

The peace of God enables us to live in peace with God, with ourselves and with our fellow man.

Romans 5:1

JUST LISTEN

One word from God – just one word – can
change everything for you. Take time out
to listen for that word today.

Ezekiel 4:7
2 Kings 20:16

LET GOD LEAD

When you surrender to Christ, you look
at life through His eyes. This enables you to
handle life through His strength.

John 14:16

SLEEP WELL!

Sleep is a gift from God. The Psalmist says: It is vain to sit up late … for so he gives up his beloved sleep. Maybe the most spiritual thing you can do right now is put this book down and take a nap!

Psalms 127:2
Ecclesiastes 5:12

LOVE ONE ANOTHER

Anything that makes it difficult to love our
fellow man makes it difficult to love God.

John 13:34
1 John 4:7

DON'T LEAVE OUT GOD

Don't get so involved in the work of God
that you neglect the God of the work!

John 15:5

A COMFORT THOUGHT

The Holy Spirit is our comforter.
Isn't that comforting to know?

John 14:16
John 14:26

PRAY

When in need, pray this prayer:
Prince of peace I need you. Take charge. I need
comfort and courage that comes from your spirit.
Let me find you in a quiet place where I can hear
your heartbeat and feel secure. Amen.

Psalms 62:8

LET PEACE FLOW

When the Holy Spirit fills your life, you
immediately become a channel of God's
love and his peace.

Psalm 37:11

CONTROL YOURSELF

'Self' will always find reasons to be dissatisfied.
Your spirit will always search for reasons
to be thankful. Both are at enmity; the winner
depends on you. Let your spirit rule.

1 Thessalonians 5:18

LEARN FROM OTHERS

Read the scriptures and see how often the
peace of God sustained and carried people
through, even Jesus Christ.

John 5:39

TRUST IN GOD

By maintaining your peace when under attack,
you're telling the Devil 'I'm still trusting in God'.
This baffles the enemy.

Ephesians 6:13

SEEK RECONCILIATION

Jesus said: When you offer your gift at the altar,
and you remember that someone has something
against you, leave your gift and go and make peace
first. It's still the best advice for reconciliation.

Matthew 5:23, 24

AMAZING GRACE

Never underestimate the glorious gift of grace.
Jesus gave his life for you and wishes to grant
you complete restoration.

Ephesians 2:8

PERFECT LOVE

Whatever your circumstances, always remember
that God loves you with an unfathomable love that
cannot be measured, and that is totally perfect.

Jeremiah 31:3
Nahum 1:7

HE THAT IS GREATER

Remember there is One greater than you,
in whom all fear dissolves.

1 John 4:4

GAIN EVERLASTING PEACE

Jesus is the same yesterday, today and forever.
This means the peace he offers is timeless.

Hebrews 13:8

CLAIM GOD'S GIFT

Peace is the gift of God.

1 John 4:18
2 Tim 1:7

AVOID DOUBT

It will surprise you how often the thing you
fear the most will never come to pass.

Deuteronomy 1:21
Matthew 21:21

GRATITUDE

Having a spirit of gratitude is like a tonic:
it smoothes the ruffled brow and places a smile
upon the countenance.

1 Samuel 12:24
Psalms 126:3

MULTIPLY YOUR BLESSINGS

There are two ways to multiply our blessings. One is to recognise them, the other is to share them.

Ephesians 1:3

REST

The way of escape that God offers us is not a
flight, but a release. He says: Come unto me
and I will give you rest.

Matthew 11:28
Exodus 20:8-11

BE FREE IN CHRIST

When you know your sins are truly forgiven,
you know you are truly free.

Galatians 5:1

LEAVE IT WITH GOD

Having turned your problem over to God, cease
worrying and go peacefully about other duties.
It is no longer your matter, but His.

Psalm 55:22

THE FUTURE IS BRIGHT WITH GOD

Worry is blind and cannot discern the future,
but God sees the end from the beginning.

Revelation 1:8

SPREAD LOVE

If feeling despondent, visit someone not as
fortunate as you. Pass on a cheery word of
comfort. I guarantee you will feel lifted too.

Galatians 6:2

USE YOUR IMAGINATION

We are told worry is what continues after a danger
is passed or before it arrives. It thrives on
imagination. Therefore fill your mind with peaceful
thoughts so there's no room for anything else.

Isaiah 26:3

ENJOY TODAY

The future is today. Live for today, enjoy today – it comes but only once.

Psalm 118:24

SWAP BAD FOR GOOD

Suppression is not a good way to deal with bad
feelings. Substitution is better. Rid yourself
of them by transferring them with encouraging
thoughts concerning God.

Ezekiel 18:31

SEEK PEACE

Follow after the things that make for peace ...
things that are true, honest and just.

Philippians 4:8
Romans 14:19

TURN SMILES INTO LAUGHTER

The ability to make someone laugh is a rare creative gift, yet it only begins with a smile.

Psalm 126:2
Proverbs 15:13

EXPRESS YOURSELF

Writing out your troubled thoughts on paper
extracts the mind of haphazard thinking.
Try doing this and experience a mental release.

Jeremiah 30:2
1 John 1:4
Revelation 1:19

BE CREATIVE

'A picture paints a thousand words'. Try expressing yourself though painting – it's a healing balm.

Philippians 4:7

BREATHE IN, BREATHE OUT

Deep rhythmic breathing is a splendid aid to relaxation. It improves circulation, frees the lungs, stimulates the brain, steadies the nerves and gives a feeling of control and poise. Try it right now.

3 John 2

AFFIRM SOMEONE

Affirmations motivate us to move forward.
Try affirming someone today by giving
a genuine word of approval.

Philippians 2:3

BE CONTENT

Learn to be content with what you have: a quiet
home; a few books of inspiration; a few
trustworthy friends; and a hundred innocent
pleasures that bring no pain or remorse.

1 Timothy 6:8

BE CHILDLIKE

Children have no thought for the past or the
future. They enjoy the moment. Follow them into
their beautiful and enchanting world.

Matthew 19:14
Psalm 127:3

FIND SOLITUDE

Solitude is much more than the mere absence of
noise or cessation of movement. In the midst
of turmoil, you can have stillness
in the secret refuge of your soul.

Psalm 23
Psalm 72:3

GET A SOUL MATE

When you come across a kindred spirit who sees
you 'eye to eye', regard the meeting as having
been brought by providence and enjoy a new
friendship. It was meant to be.

Proverbs 27:9

AVOID GLOOMY PEOPLE!

People who have gloomy moods attract
to themselves gloomy people and gloomy
people have a knack of producing gloomy
situations. Avoid them!

Proverbs 15:12, 18
Proverbs 22:24-25

LOOK FOR THE GOOD

When misfortunes arise, consider that it may
be a blessing in disguise.

Deuteronomy 28:2
Ephesians 1:3

ANGEL DELIGHT

In times of need, remember that God sends His angels to camp around those who trust Him, and to deliver them from their troubles.

Psalm 34:7

INSPIRE YOURSELF

In times of ailment very often the body will heal
itself, especially when you feed the mind with
words such as 'Be strong and of a good courage.'

Joshua 1:9

QUESTIONS, QUESTIONS

Serenity. Three phrases you should let go from
your mind if you want to be serene are 'what if?',
'if only' and 'why me?'

Proverbs 3:5, 6

ACCEPT THE BEST

You can't have the best of everything, but you
can make the best of what you've got.

1 Thessalonians 5:18

REACH FOR THE SKY

Your thoughts set the limits of your actions.
If you aim for the highest you may not reach it,
but the spot at which you do arrive may
not be far off the mark.

Proverbs 23:7

MEDICINE FOR LIFE

Our rations of adversities are really medicines
prescribed by the Great Physician for our
ultimate benefit. Each dose contains
ingredients for eternal life.

Job 23:10

GET OVER IT!

No anxiety lasts forever or even for very long.
Whatever you are going through, it, too, shall pass.

1 Peter 5:7

RESPECT YOURSELF, RESPECT OTHERS

'Do unto others as you would want them do to you'. This is the golden rule of peace.

Luke 6:31

STAY CALM

Many aches and pains are of emotional origin.
Back pain, excessive perspiration, palpitations and
ulcers: all have their root in negative emotion.
Next time you feel discomfort, check your mood.

Palm 25:18
Job 15:20
Dan 5:6

APPRECIATE YOURSELF

Note the things you are good at and concentrate
your efforts on them. Remind yourself from time
to time of your worthwhile qualities. There's
nothing wrong with self-praise.

Psalm 139:14

FIRST THINGS FIRST

The best anti-stress devise is to start your day
with prayer and meditation.

Mark 1:35

KEEP YOUR FRIENDS

Take time off for friendship. Your quality of life
can be greatly enriched by maintaining those
special ties. So will theirs.

Proverbs 17:17

THE BEST MEDICINE

Laughter will lower your blood pressure, keep
ulcers at bay, reduce your worries, tone up
your nervous system and above all make your
face more pleasant to look at!

Proverbs 17:22
Proverbs 15:13

PRAY FOR DAILY BREAD

For each new day, pray for enough strength for
that day, enough love for that day, enough hope
for that day, enough peace for that day.

Psalms 29:11

KEEP YOUR MIND CLEAN

The human mind is the most powerful healing
force in the world, not matched by any drug.
Avoid contamination by impure thoughts!

Jeremiah 4:14

HELP SOMEONE

However insignificant, try to make time for
one small act of service each day.

Ephesians 4:32

A HUG A DAY

Hugging is remedial. It ceases depression and
reduces stress. It has no unpleasant side effects
and is nothing less than a miracle drug.
Give someone a hug today!

Songs 8:3

THINK POSITIVE

We can think of only one thought at any
given time. Invariably one kind of thought
is driven out by another. You can learn to
dispel negative thinking by simply replacing
them with positive ones.

Philippians 2:6

SURRENDER

If you need reconciliation after a disagreement
with someone, try giving a peace offering.
It's a sure way of starting a truce.

Proverbs 7:14

MEDITATE

'Whatsoever things are true, whatsoever things
are lovely, and whatsoever things are honest,
think on these things.'

Philippians 4:8

WATCH OUT!

God has more for you! You haven't seen your best
days yet. There's more ahead than behind you.
So be prepared for exciting things.

Isaiah 43:18-19

CAST YOUR CARES

'Be anxious for nothing'. All it does
is distort your mind.

1 Peter 5:7

SHOWERS OF BLESSING

To the stormy winds and waves Jesus said,
'Peace be still', and there was a great calm.
He can do the same in your storms of life.

Mark 4:39

BE MADE WHOLE

God's plan is not simply to repair your brokenness;
it is to make you a new creature. That's why
He's been revealing, removing and restoring
certain things in your life.

2 Corinthians 5:17
Galatians 4:19

BE AN OVERCOMER

Jesus said: In this world you will have tribulations,
but be of good cheer, I have overcome the world.

John 16:33

BE A PEACEMAKER

Blessed are the peacemakers, for they shall
be called God's children.

Matthew 5:9

IT'S GOD'S WAY, NOT YOURS

In difficult times, God teaches us that despite our
knowledge, skills and experience to solve problems,
we only ultimately overcome 'not by might,
nor by power, but by my Spirit'.

Zechariah 4:6

PEACE IN CRISIS

Guard your inward peace, even if your
whole world is in turmoil.

Psalm 112:6
Psalm 122:7, 8

FREELY ACCEPT

Peace is one of the fruits of the spirit.
It is the evidence of a spirit-filled life. The good
news is God's spirit is free to all.

Galatians 5:22

SELF-ANALYSIS

What's blocking you from experiencing God's joy?
Find out as soon as you can and refuse
to live another day with it.

Nehemiah 8:10

LIVE GOD'S WILL

When you know you're doing God's will, you
experience a lasting pleasure that simply
can't be found anywhere else!

Matthew 7:21

LOVE YOUR NEIGHBOUR

Lets face it; sometimes confrontation does end
in permanent division. That's why 'if possible,
live peaceably with all men'.

Romans 12:18

LOOK FOR THE GOOD IN OTHERS

Compliments by their very nature are
biodegradable, and tend to dissolve hours
or days after we receive them; that is why
we can always use another.

Ephesians 4:25
Ephesians 6:8

BE AN INTERCESSOR

When God prompts you to pray for someone else, don't wait. Do it! Your prayers may be the only one thing standing between that person and catastrophe.

2 Thessalonians 3:1

ADMIT YOUR FAULTS

One step toward recovering your peace is to admit
that you are creating most of your stress.

Psalm 32:5
1 John 1:9

PRAY WITHOUT CEASING

Heaven stops to listen to your prayer. Think about that! Your thoughts, struggles and goals may not mean much to others, but they register with God.

1 Thessalonians 5:17